BOAZ IS
DEAD

& 9 Other Essential Truths
for Christian Singles

MARK MOORE, JR.

KEEN VISION PUBLISHING

Limits of Liability and Disclaimer of Warranty

Cover Design: J Designs www.jdesignsonline.com

Printed in the United States of America
ISBN 978-0-9990740-5-3
Keen Vision Publishing, LLC
www.keen-vision

CONTENTS

Introduction

I hate to be the bearer of bad news. *I really do.* Especially when it is news about someone who is so well loved by people who don't even know him. Just think about it. While there is a plethora of eligible Adams, Jasons, and Roberts, etc., all we ever hear about is Boaz. He is, without a doubt, one of the most popular men in the Bible, yet one of the most misunderstood and misrepresented. It is amazing to me that so many people who don't know where Boaz is from, what Boaz did, what Boaz looks like, and what he is interested in somehow know without a shadow of a doubt they want to either have him or be him. Depending on the generation you happen to be a part of, Boaz is the Biblical Billy Dee Williams/Denzel Washington/Idris Elba. He's the believers' Brad Pitt, the Christians' Channing Tatum, and the Saints' Steve McQueen.

Men want to be him, women want to be with him, but no one really *knows* him. In fact, Boaz is such a hot commodity that every other singles' conference or service has a Boaz inspired theme. Am I the only one who has seen the "Waiting On Boaz Conference" or the "Searching For Boaz Summit"? I didn't think so.

What makes this infatuation with Boaz so troubling, however, is the fact that most people aren't really in love with the *Boaz of the Bible*. The majority of people wanting to be him or have him are in love with the *Boaz of their subjective and varied imaginations*. And that Boaz, my friends, is dead.

Maybe you didn't receive an invite to the home going service, but he died a long time ago. He died when we attempted to make his story a romantic comedy of sorts instead of a picture of God's love towards us and a roadmap to a blessed relationship. He died when we reduced his story to one of *patience* instead of *perseverance* and *waiting* instead of *working*. The Biblical story of Boaz and Ruth is essentially a story of *commitments*, *causes*, and *connections*.

This book, Boaz is Dead, is filled with both practical and spiritual wisdom. Much like the story of Ruth & Boaz, this book is really not about Boaz at all. It is designed to not only help you identify with and relate to the one God has for you but also to become the one God wants you to be. Before we do that, however, we must bury Boaz and every misconception about this character that has migrated from generation to generation.

After reading about how perfect Boaz was for Ruth and the beauty of what they produced together, one may think, *"Shouldn't we try to resuscitate him?"* After all, I'm sure some of you are more convinced now than ever that Boaz is absolutely who you want to be like or be with. I mean, since he's the kind of man who could provide a *place*, *protection*, and *provision*, shouldn't every woman want him and every man desire to be him? No. We should learn the lessons his life teaches us, bury him, look to connect with the one God wants us to be with, and most importantly, become who God wants us to be.

The reason I make this claim is not because of the obvious fact that the literal Boaz who lived thousands of years ago is dead, but because we must lay to rest the obsession with having a relationship *just* like his. The sobering reality behind why we should let him die is the fact that he was for *Ruth*. Everything about his existence was tailor made for no one except *Ruth*. Understanding the importance of this is so fitting for us today because we tend to make ourselves the protagonist of every Biblical story. Think of it this way: Have you ever read the story of David and Goliath and *not* thought of yourself as David? Or, how about the story of Daniel in the lion's den? Have you ever *not* thought of yourself as Daniel? Surely every one of us who has visualized brave Moses on the banks of the Red Sea or fearless Peter stepping out of the boat to walk on water has never imagined ourselves as being anyone other than the hero.

As wonderful as this sounds, the reality is we aren't the hero *in* every story. Some of us are more like

David's brothers who didn't receive the oil from the horn of the prophet or one of Daniel's neighbors who wondered what would happen to his stuff since he wasn't coming back home. Others are more like one of the children of Israel who wondered how in the world Moses was going to make the waters part or one of the other disciples in the boat who secretly thought Peter was completely out of his mind. The unfortunate fact is that we aren't the hero of every story, and to be more precise, we aren't even in every story.

Don't believe me yet? Well, tell me this. As a Christian single, have you ever desired a relationship like any biblical couple other than Ruth & Boaz? Once again, I didn't think so. What must be addressed, however, is the fact that the connection of Ruth to Boaz was all about facilitating the conception of Obed. They teach us that the true beauty of and purpose for a relationship is not about how great you look together or how many people tell you the two of you make a great couple. The true beauty of a relationship lies in what it produces. Every God inspired connection is designed to produce something and scripture proves it time and time again from Adam & Eve to Abraham & Sarah, to Elizabeth & Zechariah, and to Mary & Joseph.

As singles who desire God's best, we must pray that He connects us with those who are equipped to produce that in which we're partially responsible for developing. Therefore, we must realize Ruth and Boaz may not really be our relationship goal. While it's the stereotypical relationship in scripture, it's not the only one. Some of our relationships should be like Abraham and Sarah who ultimately produced a nation after years of battling seemingly unfulfilled promises and infertility. Some of us should be like Mary and Joseph who raised God in the flesh, although it literally required an angelic visitation to keep their relationship together. Some of you may be the woman at the well who don't need to meet Boaz, but right now you need to meet Jesus. Some of the men reading this may feel bad because unlike Boaz, you're not established and independently wealthy, but you're driven like Jacob and willing to work for who you believe God has for you. Wherever we are in our journey, our goal should ultimately be to connect with who *we* need. To put this in perspective, for those who are supposed to be married, you don't need a spouse, you need *your* spouse. One of the worst things that could happen would be for you to miss what you *need* while trying to get what Ruth *had*.

There are two important lessons we must learn from Ruth & Boaz's interaction before we move on to the other truths contained in this book. The first one is that everyone won't get married...and that's ok. Yes, you did read what you think you read. Marriage is not an indication of your worth. Your lack of a ring is not synonymous with a lack of value. Before you accuse me of simply trying to hurt your feelings, understand that I am not necessarily saying *you* won't get married, but I am saying that *everybody* (including some of those who are considered eligible) won't get married. Mathematics support my claim. Whether we want to agree with it or not, worldwide census information is clear in telling us there are more women than men. Spend some time with that thought. Has it hit you yet? The fact that there are more women than men suggests that even if we lined all the men in the world next to all the women in the world and paired them off two by two, there would be leftovers. We'll deal with this more later on, but suffice it to say that even though everyone may not get married, everyone *can* be happy.

The production our relationships should aim for is not limited to physical enjoyment. This applies to potentially romantic and platonic relationships. Every connection we make should be geared towards producing something greater than ourselves. Whether it's mutual encouragement, a business idea, or even just a commitment to keep each other lifted in prayer, something productive should come out of it.

As we move forward, be open to receiving who God has for you and also becoming who God wants you to be. No, you can't have Boaz because he's dead. In fact, Abraham, Moses, David, Solomon, Peter, James, and John are dead too. The good news, however, is that your destiny is yet alive, and so is Vernon, Nigel, Odell, Scott, Brandon, & Richard and one of them may be just what you need to facilitate your destiny. Let's let Ruth and Boaz have their happily ever after, I promise God knows how to give you your own.

Chapter One
Boaz is Dead

"And he said unto me, "Son of man, can these bones live?" And I said, "No, Lord. That's Boaz...let him stay dead."

II Mark 17:29

I f we were to conduct a survey and ask random believers for information about Boaz, I believe we would notice some similarity in responses. Many would suggest that he was strikingly handsome, rich, youthful, employed, and faithful. Unfortunately, that is where many of the similarities would end because the rest of our perspectives on Boaz are based solely on our personal preferences. Ladies who like their men tall, dark, and handsome envision him being tall, dark and handsome. Those who like their men bald envision a bald Boaz. Ladies who like smooth Jazz see Boaz with a saxophone in his hand and sunglasses on his face. In fact, so many people project their personal preferences on him that there are endless descriptions of what he actually looks like.

While thoughts on his appearance may change based on the individual, and there are certain general characteristics that are commonly accepted about his financial status and character. There is one attribute that is almost universally assigned to him, and that is Boaz is to be waited on. While this idea is widely circulated, it is incredibly flawed because no one should be left waiting on a dead man.

IT'S NOT EVEN ABOUT HIM

To fully understand this position, you must first understand the actual story of Ruth. It's interesting to note that while Boaz gets most of the attention, the story isn't really about him at all; it's really about Ruth. In fact, the book is named after her. The Bible informs us in Ruth 1 that she is the daughter-in-law of a woman by the name of Naomi. Naomi and her husband, Elimelech, were forced to leave their homeland in Judah as a result of a famine that had come to the land, and they settled in Moab. They had two sons, Mahlon and Chilion, who married wives while in Moab. This is where we are formerly introduced to Ruth and her sister-in-law, Orpah.

Unfortunately, all three of the men in Naomi's life, her husband and sons, died unexpectedly and left Naomi, Ruth, and Orpah as widows.

This is where the story takes a significant turn and highlights a few of the attributes that make Ruth such a dynamic figure and position her to meet Boaz. After the death of her sons and husband, Naomi received word that the famine that had caused them to leave her homeland had ended. Naomi then decided it would best for her to head back to Judah. It is important that we view this story through the cultural lens of the day. During these Biblical days, a man was more than an accessory in the life of a woman. He represented security, provision, and stability. With this in mind, remember that Naomi has lost her husband and her sons while Ruth and Orpah have lost their husbands. In essence, no husbands meant the three of them were completely uncovered and unprotected.

Being the unselfish woman that she was, Naomi had a heart-to -heart conversation with Ruth and Orpah concerning their future. She attempted to be considerate of their plight and release them to return to Moab and the families they left when they married her sons. This decision, on the part of Naomi, was designed to give them a chance in a society where a husband was considered a necessary component if any quality of life was to be enjoyed. After the option going back home had presented itself, a tale of two women unfolds.

Orpah, who like Ruth was a Moabite, seized the opportunity to go back home. In all actuality, you would be hard pressed to find anything wrong with her decision. Think about this for a moment, Orpah had left her homeland and her kindred to follow her husband and even opted to stay with her mother-in-law after his death. Who could fault her for wanting to return to the land of her birth and the potential security of her homeland?

Ruth, on the other hand, provided a very different response. When Naomi presented the opportunity to return to Moab, which was both a selfless act on her part and the sensible choice for her daughters-in-law, she had no way of knowing Ruth would give the response she did. Instead of following the same path Orpah had taken and opting to return to Moab, Ruth instead pledged her allegiance and loyalty to Naomi. Let's take a look at the account in Ruth 1: 16-17 (NIV):

"Where you go I will go, and where you stay I will stay. Your people will be my people and your God my God. Where you die I will die, and there I will be buried."

It is this single declaration of commitment, as a result of her character, not a physical feature or an academic accomplishment, that positioned Ruth to receive everything that God had in store for her.

What Have You Committed Yourself To?

While Ruth is clearly a woman, the principles she embodied apply to both men and women. There are so many lessons found in her story, but we should all take note of the way her commitment factored into her ultimate destiny. Ruth's decision to stay with Naomi was more than simply providing companionship to an older woman, but rather she committed herself to a cause that was bigger than her. The tone of her response to Naomi's suggestion doesn't reveal the heart of someone undecided about their position or simply willing to "give it a try." On the contrary, her response expressed the unwavering resolve of someone completely sure of his/ her decision and willing to remove the very possibility of turning back. She didn't tell Naomi, *"I will stick with you a little while longer."* or, *"Let me see how I feel in the morning."* but she essentially told her, *"Wherever you go, wherever you stay, and whoever you worship, I will be there with you."*

This kind of commitment is essential to our understanding of both this story and our relationships because it presents us with an opportunity to consider our commitments and the way our character has influenced them. Before we are ready to meet anyone, it is important that we have first identified a cause that is worthy of making a "Ruth level" commitment to. If we are not careful, we can be so eager to be connected with someone that we fail to first find something that's worth sticking with.

With this in mind, ask yourself these two questions:

- What have I committed to?
- What God-given mandate have I obligated to fulfill, even if I must do it alone?

I am not at all suggesting that you must make the same commitment that Ruth made of following a person around, but I am suggesting there should be something bigger than you that you're working towards achieving. What promises have you made to yourself? What promises have you made to your family? What have you committed to that will impact the generation to come? In other words, what are you working on? Maybe you're committed to advancing the cause of the Gospel among those who you have influence with or building a business that has the potential to sustain future generations. Whatever it is, you must make sure you are about something that is bigger than just being found by someone or finding someone to make you happy. **You aren't ready to connect with anyone until you've first connected to a sense of purpose and individual identity.**

At this particular juncture in the story, Ruth has committed to taking care of Naomi. This was indeed something far greater than herself, seeing that she didn't have the power or the wherewithal to do this on her own. What we soon discover, however, is that **the right commitments will always lead to the right connections.** Upon arriving in Judah, things began to work in Ruth's favor. During this time, it was customary for harvesters to allow the poor, widows, and orphans to glean in the grain fields during the time of harvest. This meant that those who did not have the ability to care or provide for themselves could follow behind the workers in the fields and collect the leftovers or that which was dropped so they would have something to eat. In an effort to honor her commitment to care for Naomi, Ruth asked if she could find a field to glean from. After receiving Naomi's blessing to do so, she set out in hopes of finding the perfect field that would provide them with enough sustenance to survive. Unbeknownst to Ruth, the field she began to work in belonged to a wealthy older man named Boaz, who we later learn is Naomi's relative from her late husband's side of the family.

Consider this for a moment: The book of Ruth is only four chapters long, but we aren't even introduced to Boaz until chapter 2. Isn't that a powerful lesson in and of itself? Half of our ideal love story should really take place before we even meet the person we've been praying for. This should certainly serve as consolation to those of you who feel discouraged by the fact that you haven't met anyone who appears suitable. The good news is that the foundation for the relationship you desire is being laid through the decisions you make right now. This is why we must not overlook the importance of developing the kind of Godly character that leads us to commit to the right things. What we are committed to determines what (and who) we are positioned to connect with.

Ruth arrived in Boaz's field early one morning, unaware of who it belonged to, and began to work gathering grain. Late that afternoon, Boaz showed up, saw Ruth, and then asked the overseer of his workers a very crucial question. In Ruth 2:7, Boaz asks, *"Who does that young women belong too?"* It would be very easy for us to romanticize this conversation. I'll admit that for a long time, I actually did. I envisioned Boaz riding up on his regal black charger in slow motion and spotting the beautiful Ruth standing tall among the wheat and smiling at him before slowly throwing her long, flowing hair over her shoulders. I envisioned him hopping off his horse, pulling one of his workers aside, and, in a tone that was both nervous and optimistic, asking, *"Who is that beautiful woman I can't seem to take my eyes off of?!"* In my mind, this was a "love at first sight" moment, but in reality, that's not how it happened. The cultural context suggests something entirely different.

You see, Boaz was not a young Romeo, he was an old businessman. The inquiry he made to his foreman about Ruth's identity was more about protecting his property than it was about making a love connection. What he was really asking was, "Who is this lady in my field that I've never seen before? Where does she come from and who does she belong to?" Keep in mind that he had never seen her before. Ruth was a foreigner in Judah, a Moabite woman who couldn't help but to stand out. The answer the foreman provided is extremely insightful and contains information that everyone who desires to be in a relationship should take note of. The foreman told Boaz that Ruth was the Moabite who came back with Naomi. She had asked early that morning if she could glean in the field. He then informed him that she had been working faithfully all day and had barely even taken a break.

Up until this point, Boaz has said nothing to Ruth; he has only questioned her presence in his field. After hearing the report of his foreman, however, he then turned and spoke directly to Ruth. He offered her three things that spark the turn of events in her life. In fact, the way the Bible explains it is so perfect, I want you to read it for yourself.

"So Boaz said to Ruth, "My daughter, listen to me. Don't go and glean in another field and don't go away from here. Stay here with the women who work for me. Watch the field where the men are harvesting, and follow along after the women. I have told the men not to lay a hand on you. And whenever you are thirsty, go and get a drink from the water jars the men have filled."

Ruth 2: 8-9 NIV

Do you see it for yourself? He first told her not to go anywhere else. Then, he told her that he had instructed his men not to lay a hand on her. Finally, he informed her that she had access to the fresh water his men had provided. Boaz showed Ruth that he was both willing and able to provide her with a place, protection, and provisions. The preacher in me is just dying to park here and drive this point home, but I haven't reached my destination yet. He went from not even speaking to her directly to providing her with everything she needed. What led to this change? It wasn't just her looks or the way he felt when he saw her. If that were the case, he would have spoken to her directly as soon as he arrived in the field. The question of why Boaz decided to be so kind to Ruth is such a good one that even Ruth posed this question.

"At this, she bowed down with her face to the ground. She asked him, "Why have I found such favor in your eyes that you notice me—a foreigner?"

Ruth 2:10 (NIV)

Ruth was so blown away by his kind overtures that she had to question the reason for Boaz's kindness. His response to Ruth provides timeless insight singles can still use today.

"Boaz replied, 'I've been told all about what you have done for your mother-in-law since the death of your husband—how you left your father and mother and your homeland and came to live with a people you did not know before.'"

Ruth 2:11 (NIV)

Boaz revealed that his kindness had nothing to do with her, but everything to do with her commitment to his cousin Naomi. His decision to look out for Ruth came directly on the heels of learning that she was both connected to and providing for Naomi. Ruth's destiny connected to her because she had enough character to honor her commitment. She did not know that the field she entered that morning belonged to the cousin of the one she had vowed to support. She did not know she wouldn't be turned away or harmed by competitors while working there. She did not know the consistency of her work would be noticed by those around her and subsequently reported to those with the power to reward it. What she did know, however, was that gleaning in a field and finding something to eat was directly linked to her commitment to care for Naomi, and she was determined to honor that by any means necessary.

Could it be that part of the reason you're frustrated in your singleness is because you haven't developed enough character to make commitments worthy of the right connection yet? Is it possible that while you are working like Ruth, your work is strictly based on a desire to be found instead of a desire to do something that makes a difference and honors God?

While I'm asking questions, let me also ask you to consider what would have happened if Ruth had made the same choice as Orpah. How would her life have been different if in the middle of that dusty road she had opted to take the easy route? The best possible answers to both questions are found in examining the fruit produced as a result of the decision she chose to make.

Matthew's Gospel records the genealogy of Jesus and gives account of the 42 generations that led to the birth of our savior.

"Salmon the father of Boaz, whose mother was Rahab, Boaz the father of Obed, whose mother was Ruth, Obed the father of Jesse, and Jesse the father of King David."

Matthew 1:5-6 (NIV)

Do any of those names look familiar? In the genealogy of the Savior of the world, we find Ruth, Boaz and their son, Obed. The same Obed who fathered Jesse who fathered King David who ultimately led to the birth of Jesus Christ. These two short verses at the beginning of the New Testament are there to show us that everything that transpired between Ruth and Boaz was centered around what they would conceive.

The relationship between Ruth and Boaz is not the boy meets girl romance we have made it out to be, nor is it the exact template that every relationship must follow. It is, however, an excellent example of the path to purpose that all Christian singles should follow.

Character influences commitments, commitments shape connections, and connections determine conception.

Chapter Two
Equally Yoked

"Behold, how good and how pleasant it is for two people who are dating to actually match."

II Mark 1:7

Research suggests that even though we have easier access to information than ever before, our generation is arguably the most Biblically illiterate generation that the world has ever seen. Even in light of this troubling information, I can assure you that there are several scriptures that at least all Christian singles know by heart. You would be hard pressed to find one that isn't familiar with the following...

The "I must get married, or I'll burst into flames" Scripture...
"But if they cannot control themselves, they should marry, for it is better to marry than to burn with passion."

I Corinthians 7:9 (NIV)

The "I can't do that because I belong to God" Scripture...
"Therefore, I urge you, brothers and sisters, in view of God's mercy, to offer your bodies as a living sacrifice, holy and pleasing to God--this is your true and proper worship."

Romans 12:1 (NIV)

The "I can't get married in Heaven, so I need to hurry and marry now" Scripture...

"At the resurrection people will neither marry nor be given in marriage; they will be like the angels in heaven."

Matthew 22:30 (NIV)

While the overwhelming majority of Christian singles are familiar with the scripture references above, there is another one we must mention and focus on because it is most commonly misunderstood.

The Apostle Paul poses a question in 2nd Corinthians 6:14 that baffles many of us: *"Be ye not unequally yoked together with unbelievers: for what fellowship hath righteousness with unrighteousness? And what communion hath light with darkness?"*

This particular scripture is so crucial because, in many ways, it is viewed as the litmus test that determines whether or not a possible suitor is qualified or not. As straightforward and simple as it sounds, it forces us to raise several questions, primarily, "What does it actually mean?" The notion of being "equally yoked" is somewhat controversial because so many people have their own interpretation of what Paul's meaning. The widespread consensus that most people agree on, however, is that the essence of the statement is basically an admonition to avoid connecting or entering a relationship with someone who is not on the same level (more specifically, the same spiritual level) as you are.

If we were to poll the average Christian single, or anyone for that matter, and ask them to interpret what the Scripture means, there would be mixed responses. Some would say that the scripture's message is limited to warning believers against marrying people who aren't of like faith. Others would argue that it applies to the stages of a relationship that come before marriage like dating and even friendship. Then, of course, there is the argument of what constitutes an "unbeliever." Are they an unbeliever if they don't have the same doctrinal positions as you? Are they an unbeliever if they believe in a God but don't believe in your God? Should they be classified as an unbeliever if they don't go to church consistently?

DO THEY REALLY BELIEVE?

We could debate what an "unbeliever" actually is all day, but I think that there are two fundamental questions that every Christian single can use as a guide when determining if the person they are considering is a believer or not.

1. Do they agree on WHO God is?

As simple as it sounds, this is the foundational question we should all ask before pursuing a relationship with someone and especially a relationship that has the potential to be romantic in nature. The fact of the matter is that everyone is a believer of and in something, but the question becomes, *"What do they believe about God?"* This is the foundation on which everything else will be built. It is important that this question is not skipped over. I can't tell you how many times I have seen people skip over this foundational step in an effort to force something to happen, but this never works in the long run. If the two of you can't agree on who God is, then there is no foundation on which to build anything substantive. Do you have the same views on salvation? Do you share the same views on what being "saved" looks like? It important that we enter relationships with our eyes wide open and a willingness to ask questions.

2.   Do they agree on WHAT role He plays in not just relationships, but in life in general?

This question goes hand in hand with the previous question, but it further reveals the depth of their spiritual nature. You will run into problems if you are someone who desires to acknowledge God in all of your ways, but you're trying to make a relationship work with someone who just sees God as an "every other Sunday" obligation.

If they can't pass these simple tests on belief, it doesn't make sense to go any further.

These are just a few of the questions that emerge from this conversation, but it is my opinion that the total significance of the scripture must not be limited to simply the last part of the first clause that deals with unbelievers. To fully understand the meaning of this verse, we must put equal emphasis on the first clause that introduces the notion of being equally yoked.

This imagery is not as readily understandable to those of us in this 21st century, technology-driven society, but keep in mind that it was written to people who were accustomed to an agricultural economy. There were no supermarkets or big box stores for them to purchase groceries or provisions. They survived with the assistance of agriculture. For this reason, the idea of being "equally yoked" would have immediately resonated with them.

In short, the phrase spoke to the farmers' routine of yoking or placing two oxen in the same harness for the purpose of plowing a specific field together. What is most interesting to note, however, is that the common practice was not to join the two strongest oxen together in the same yoke. Think about this for a moment. It would appear that pairing oxen that were equal in strength and experience was the more practical thing to do, however, common practice was to join a stronger and more mature ox with a younger and less experienced ox so that one could teach the other.

How does this impact our understanding of Paul's admonishing us to avoid being unequally yoked with unbelievers? For starters, it shows us that being "equally yoked" doesn't necessarily mean that both of you have the same amount of experience, skills, or abilities. How many people have missed out on God connections because of a misunderstanding of what being equally yoked means? The master's decision to yoke two oxen was not limited to how similar they were, but it was influenced by his belief that they could move in the same direction to accomplish the same purpose. Don't misunderstand my premise, shared interest and commonality is essential (as we will emphasize later), but the real test of the legitimacy of the yoking is in shared direction. It's interesting to note that the purpose of the yoke being placed around the neck of the oxen was to limit their ability to be distracted by looking around at their surroundings. The yoke kept them focused on what was in front of them. Do you see the significance of this as it pertains to our relationships? One way to know if you are equally yoked is to look at your willingness to focus on the same goals and head in the same direction. Too many Christian relationships crumble because while there is shared belief, there is no agreement on purpose and direction which apply to more than just the spiritual dimension of our relationships.

Can I be honest? Of course, I can. It's my book. I am consistently blown away by the puzzled expressions and replies I receive when certain people learn that I am still single. "But Mark, you travel a lot. SURELY you meet sweet saved young ladies all of the time." Or, "Mark, what's wrong with *Insert random Church girl with a long skirt and a smile*?! She loves The Lord! Look at how she worships." If only it were that simple. We must remember that being equally yoked is more than just shared belief about God, but also shared belief about direction and purpose. With this in mind, it is impossible to share direction and purpose if we only emphasize the spiritual side of our personalities and our "church façade." For example, you can't tell if you share direction and purpose with someone if the only criteria you use to determine their eligibility is whether they clap on the 2 and 4, how fluently they speak in tongues, and how many praise break videos they appear in on YouTube. Having those things in common might make the two of you excellent partners for the praise Olympics, but it doesn't necessarily translate to a sure-fire recipe for relationship success.

Think of it in these terms. Depending on the church tradition you are a part of and the level of involvement you have at your local assembly, most of us find ourselves in church two to three days per week. While we are in church two to three days a week, those who are married or in a committed relationship are in it seven days a week! Think about that. So, what makes you think that the only quality that matters in your potential spouse is how well you two interact at church?

Hear me very carefully. Being equally yoked means more than loving Jesus and Hezekiah Walker songs. As unpopular as it may sound, there are a lot of great men and women who love God but would make you miserable in a relationship because a love for God is all that you share. Do you share similar tastes in food or fashion? Are you both fully persuaded that bathing should take place at least once a day? Do the two of you see eye to eye as it pertains to the desire for and the plan on raising children?

By no means am I suggesting that a relationship can't work if the two of you don't share the same views on everything. I am suggesting that it won't work if you don't enter the relationship at least knowing that your views are different. Again, authentic belief in God is the foundation that must be present before any substantive relationship can be built. As crucial as this step is, that's exactly what it is, a step. After ensuring that you are on the same spiritual footing as the person whose attention you have captured, you must make sure that you share things in common outside of the sanctuary. One of the worst things that could happen is for you to fall in love with someone you only like at church but can't stand anywhere else.

Can we go deeper for a moment? While spiritual compatibility is the foundation for a relationship that desires "equally yoked" status and shared interest is the next step towards that goal, the most crucial element to being truly equally yoked lies in shared purpose and direction. It is possible to have two people who both love God, have many things in common, but just aren't meant to be in a relationship. Guess what? That's okay. You aren't intended to date everyone with whom you have chemistry. Some people are intended to be your friends.

The beauty of the imagery of being equally yoked is that it shows us we should look to find someone who shares purpose and direction. It's crucial that we make the distinction between our souls being yoked and our souls being tied. They both speak of connection, but the emphasis of being yoked is shared purpose while the emphasis of being tied is shared pleasure. **Yoking is for breakthrough while tying is for bondage.** We will deal with the nature of soul ties later, but suffice it to say that if you want to be equally yoked with the one God has assigned for you to pursue purpose with, it will not work if your soul is still tied to something else.

Many Christians have entered into relationships with the wrong people because they thought that the evidence of their compatibility was in the fact that they both believed and had certain similarities. We must come to grips with the fact that it takes more than just a few shared interests and a mutual belief in God to make a relationship work.

Chapter Three
Get Real

"Unrealistic expectations may endure for a night, but you should wake up by the morning."

II Mark 3:29

I already know. If this were Twitter, this chapter wouldn't get any retweets. If this were Facebook, it wouldn't get any shares. And, if it were Instagram it certainly wouldn't get any likes. This chapter presents a possibility most singles never want to consider. Simply put, this chapter bursts bubbles and shatters dreams because it forces singles to confront the fact that sometimes, some of the people we want are very much out of our league. That's right. You read that correctly...out of your league.

I'm well aware that this notion contradicts much of the modern-day logic that suggests everyone can be anything they want to be or have anything/anyone they want to have. Please make sure you understand my position. I am a firm believer that people have a God-given ability to play a role in shaping their destiny. I don't believe anyone should be limited by the circumstances surrounding their birth, their ethnicity, socio-economic status, or even gender. Do you desire to be one of the top surgeons in the nation? The fact that you were born poor shouldn't stop you from achieving that. Is it your goal to ascend to the position of CEO of a major Fortune 500 company? Great! You should not be blocked from doing that because you're a woman. Do you plan to start a non-profit organization that focuses on providing clean drinking water to those impoverished on the continent of Africa? That's amazing! Your skin color shouldn't stand in the way of you accomplishing that. The only thing that has the power to stop us from reaching our desired goals in life is our choices.

The choices we make (or don't make) serve as a predictor of our success far more than our goals, intentions, or even the strength of our personality combined. Our choices, more than even our fears, have the ability to hinder our progress. Choices can disqualify or distinguish us, plateau or propel us, and develop or destroy us. Let's revisit the examples above for just a moment. While your desire to be a top surgeon shouldn't be hindered by your family's socioeconomic status, if you chose not to go to medical school, your desire will not come true. Your goal of becoming the CEO of a Fortune 500 company shouldn't be halted by your gender, but if you choose to get three neck tattoos and four facial piercings, you may be in direct opposition to the corporate culture you desire to engage. A desire to provide clean drinking water to impoverished nations in Africa is beyond commendable, but if you never choose to obtain your passport or make contacts on the continent, your plan may not manifest.

So, how do our choices impact our relationships? That's a wonderful question. In the same way that our choices influence our opportunities for advancement and promotion in the corporate world, they also play a role in determining the quality and caliber of the relationships we will attract. In other words, our choices play a role in determining if our expectations are unrealistic or not.

Many individuals seeking to be in a relationship fail to factor in their choices when determining who or how to pursue someone. It doesn't matter how many romantic comedies we watch that attempt to convince us that we can be with whomever we want regardless of our qualifications or the feelings of the other party, we cannot get around the fact that the choices we make factor in to how we are perceived. When we fail to consider this, we are on the verge of drifting into a land of unrealistic expectations because the choices we've made sometimes trump the desires we have.

ARE YOU READY?

Consider this for a moment, as unpopular as it may sound, there is a very important question that every single need to ask themselves before beginning to pursue anyone. That question is this:

"If today was the day that I met the person I've been praying about for years...why would they want me?"

I DID tell you that this chapter would anger some of you, right? Well, okay then. Think about it. Why would THEY want YOU? Seriously, spend some time with that question. What do you have to offer? What do you love to do that coincides with their interests and passions? What values do you hold dear that they're equally committed to? What element of your vision excites them? What have you achieved that goes hand in hand with their primary purpose in life? Maybe these questions are too deep. Let's try some more entry-level inquiries. What is their favorite color? Do you two like the same types of music? Do you both possess the same sociopolitical views? Are you their physical type? Better yet...do you even know? If not, explain to me what criteria you have used to determine if the two of you would be a good match?

Chances are if you're like many other singles are today, your answer to that is strictly selfish. You feel that the two of you would be a great match simply because they fit your description of what an ideal partner looks like. They are the size, shade, and shape you like and they can provide the salary, status, and security you want. I'm glad you know what you want, but at what point do you ask yourself if you have what the person you desire wants.

We are such a self-centered generation that we never take the time to shift the focus off what we want in a relationship and place it on what we can provide in a relationship. If we were to begin to focus on what we can provide, we would realize that some of our desires have gone unfulfilled because they are simply unrealistic. Expecting someone to be with you simply because you want to be with them is unrealistic. Expecting someone to want to be with you because you monitor their social media pages all the time is borderline creepy...and unrealistic. Don't lose hope just yet. While asking ourselves why the person we desire would want us back is extremely important, there are two things it is **not** meant to suggest:

1. No one wants you.

Keep in mind that the question you need to ask yourself is not "...*why would anyone want me?*" but rather "...*why would they want me?*" I believe that it deserves mentioning that everyone has something to offer to someone else, just not necessarily the person we want, and that's okay. Your inability to attract "*them*" does not mean you're a bad person, but it can mean that you're an unrealistic person.

The choices we have made and continue to make are so absolutely crucial to our relationship success. They position us in the eyes of our potential partners and provide a frame of reference for them to use in determining if we are as good of a fit for them as we think they are for us. These choices are a reflection of our decision-making, preferences, standards (or lack thereof) and convictions. It's easier to understand it if we look at it from a different perspective and place ourselves on the other side of the equation. For example, you monitor the choices of the person you're interested in to determine just how deep your level of interest goes. Keep in mind that everything you see when you look at them is indicative of the choices they make. If you like how they dress, what they're interested in, or what they drive, for example, you're actually assessing choices they've made. On the flip side, if you don't like how they smell, whom they've dated in the past, or how they treat people, you're once again assessing their choices.

It is so easy to see the power of this when we are looking at others, but it's amazing how easy it is to disregard it when the same scrutiny is being applied to us. One of the things that always baffles me is the tendency of some to believe that desire must be reciprocated. Ironically enough, factoring the spiritual element into this equation often makes things far worse. The reason for this is because a toxic cocktail of

Biblical illiteracy and pop psychology have convinced many ill-informed believers that God owes them the person they want. After all, the BIBLE says (that statement always follows a statement that you're not supposed to argue with) *"if we ask anything in His name...He's contractually obligated to do it"*...or something like that.

As grossly misinterpreted as that "attempted" scripture is, it expresses a belief that many have that God has to give you whatever (or whoever) you want because He loves you, but that is simply not the case. Here's why. While it goes without saying that God loves us and desires to bless us, we have to realize that He is not simply our father, but He is everyone's father. This means that He cares about their well-being just as much as your well-being. In other words, why would God punish one of His children with someone they don't want just to make another one happy?

While it is the epitome of selfishness and immaturity to expect God to make someone else that He loves unhappy for the sole purpose of pleasing us, the selfishness doesn't end there. If we view both our platonic and romantic relationships as connections that are supposed to be mutually beneficial, what does it say about our character or supposed "love" for someone else if you would willingly pursue them for your benefit knowing that the cost of your gratification was their misery? Again, we must keep at the forefront of the discussion that our expectations don't have to permanently be unrealistic, but if we aren't willing to have an honest conversation about where we are at this particular time as it pertains to preparation, they most likely will. What would be tragic is for us to miss out on a wonderful relationship because we are too preoccupied with trying to force something to work with someone who isn't interested in what we have to offer.

2. You should not have standards.

It would be easy for you to read my words and take them to mean that I'm admonishing you to simply settle for what and whoever comes your direction or reaches you first. This couldn't be further from the truth. I firmly agree that every believer who happens to be single should be well aware of what they are looking for in a relationship. In the same way that we should have not only clear goals and defined desires for our career, finances, and health among other important areas of our lives, we should carry that same approach into our relationships.

You must possess a clear understanding of what you're looking for in a relationship. If you don't, you will have no idea when you find it. This understanding can be best explained and defined as what we commonly refer to as standards. Let me be as clear as possible: Standards are a wonderful thing to possess.

The standards we set determine who we give our time and attention to because they are the foundation for our attraction as well as an indicator of what we are willing to tolerate. If we were to view them as the line by which every potential partner must measure up to to receive consideration, we would understand how crucial they are because they protect us from disappointment, devastation, and disgust. With this in mind, when I ask you to consider why the person you would want would want you back, I am not at all advocating for an abandonment of standards. What I am doing is asking you to examine not only the nature of your standards but also the fairness of them. The fact of the matter is that many singles believe in what I call "one-way standards" or in other words standards that apply to everyone else...but them.

Have you seen what I'm talking about in action? If not, let's see if we can provide you with an image of what this looks like.

There is absolutely nothing wrong having certain physical qualities you would like your potential partner to have. It is absolutely your prerogative to have a preference of height, weight, occupation, age, financial status, family pedigree, style, spiritual development and more. Quite frankly, you really don't even have to explain your preferences to anyone either. Brother, if you like your sisters a little hefty then that's between you, the God you serve, and the plus-sized queen who has captured your heart. Sisters, if you like your brothers bald, dark, and handsome, I pray you find the nicest milk dud head in the kingdom. While both of these examples are strictly physical in nature, you can apply the same example to the financial, social, and spiritual standards and preferences we have. They are your preferences and, by virtue of that fact, everybody doesn't have to share them. This, however, is where we must do a little bit of self- evaluation.

If confronted about the standards you have set, I am relatively certain you would make no excuse for desiring what you desire and having a certain level of expectation as it pertains to what any interested person would have to offer to garner your attention. It is out of this realization that a hard question emerges, namely, "Am I willing to be held to the same standard I hold others to?"

Spend some time with that question. Don't say I didn't warn you that it's a tough one. Your initial knee-jerk reaction would be to immediately express how open you are to the idea of receiving the same level of scrutiny you put others through, but is that actually accurate? Are you really open to being analyzed and critiqued for the choices you've made? The reason I ask is that while many would verbally express that they have no problem with it, actions speak louder than words. I can't tell you how many times I have seen these "one-way standards" revealed on social media or in conversation. If you've been paying attention, I am certain you have seen them too. One of the main indicators of this is the argument that some people are shallow or too preoccupied with outside or material factors when selecting a mate. Naturally, our initial response to that is to agree because there are many who could justifiably be classified as shallow and that is certainly not a positive thing. What serves as the dividing line between those who are secretly expressing one-way standards and those who are legitimately highlighting shallowness is the motive and position of the person making the claim. Think through this with me for a moment. Often, the reason a person expresses disdain for a particular person's shallowness is because they have been denied by that person on the basis of not meeting their standards. Don't worry...I brought examples.

If his preference is to be with someone who has a college degree, it would be easy for a woman who is interested in him but does not have a college degree to accuse him of being shallow. If her standards demand that her suitor has at least 30 of the suggested 32 teeth in his mouth, then when she rebuffs a gentleman with 14 teeth, we could denounce her for being shallow. In other words, it's only considered shallow when we are on the receiving end of it.

If we were to flip the roles, however, we would see that one person's shallowness is another person's standard. This is where hypocrisy can come into the equation. How is it that you can have an alphabetically and categorically organized list of all the things your potential partner has to be, yet you take offense at the idea of them having standards for you? If you're not shallow for wanting her to drive a BMW, then how is she shallow for wanting you to move out of your parents' home before being considered? You expect him to be in full competitive body-building shape to even approach you, but he's shallow for having the audacity to at least want you to have a gym membership?

Who is going to jump through hoops to meet your standards and not expect you to meet any of theirs? It's this same flawed logic behind some of the popular social media "wisdom" that makes arguments like, "if they don't want you at your worst, they don't deserve you at your best" which only makes sense if you don't think about it. Why would anyone want your best if you consistently show them your worst?! Having standards is necessary to the success of any relationship, but so is being willing to embrace the fact that there are standards for you to meet.

While we see unrealistic expectations manifest in the pursuit of relationships, if we do not have the proper conversations beforehand, they can manifest within the relationship. After capturing the attention of the person we have desired, it is imperative to realize the importance of clear, realistic expectations. Open and honest dialogue prevents unrealistic expectations from evolving into confusion surrounding the roles that each party is expected to play in the relationship. One of the easiest ways to avoid this is by refusing to be so intoxicated by the thrill of courtship that you fail to properly represent yourself and your viewpoints. It is relatively easy (albeit deceitful) to fall so deeply into the rhythm of relationship that you begin to go with the proverbial flow to avoid possibly slowing down the progress that the two of you have made...even if the flow is taking you away from your true self. How many of you have experienced the uncomfortable feeling of being so intrigued by the potential of a certain relationship that you found yourself rationalizing expectations that you didn't fully agree with just to see if you could make it work? Can I get a show of hands? Raise them a little higher, please. Okay, thank you.

Almost all of us have at least been tempted to misrepresent ourselves or our views to give something we thought we wanted a fighting chance at survival. Believe me, this never works out in the long run. The reason for this is simple. If you change your viewpoints to get into a relationship, you will have to maintain your deception to stay in the relationship. Because of this, the best thing to do is to be forthright in the beginning and encourage clear communication about what the relationship is actually supposed to look like once it's been formed. What are the expectations for each person's contribution financially? Do you both agree on who the primary breadwinner will be if the relationship evolves into marriage? Are you both on the same page as it pertains to travel schedules and quality time? What about children? Have you discussed and then factored in the role that each parent would play in raising them? The answers to these questions cannot be assumed. They must be clearly discussed.

I am not at all suggesting what roles each party has to play because that is a decision that should be made by the two of you with the aid of wise counsel and the direction of the Word of God. I am suggesting that whatever the roles in the relationship are, they are known and agreed upon by both parties. The role that has been assigned for or assumed by you will not work if you are not willing to fill it.

WHO'S DOING WHAT?

I will never forget learning the importance of clear relationship roles with the help of a young lady who had attracted my interest. As a result of ministry travel and a strong social media presence, I crossed paths with a young woman I felt possessed a lot of the qualities I desire in a spouse. Based on the knowledge that I had when I met her, she was spiritually sound, physically attractive, family oriented, and educationally balanced. Needless to say, I was more than willing to pursue her further based on the surface information of which I was aware. If the surface were enough for me, I would have never encountered any red flags. Fortunately, I began to ask questions before I allowed my heart to get too involved. The more I began to ask questions, the more I began to realize that she and I did not share the same perspectives on what roles we would play in the relationship.

It is so crucial to the success of any relationship that you do not become stuck with surface level questions that only cover the basics. Knowing their favorite color or food and how many bathrooms their dream home has is great, but it does little to aide you in getting to know the real them. I began to ask more leading questions about her ideology and views on family structure that couldn't be answered with just a simple yes or no. What I discovered didn't simply trouble me, but it disqualified her. The more conversations we had, it became abundantly clear that her opinions of what life should look like did not match mine at all. Without going into too much detail and telling you all of my business (I don't know you like that), I will share that the primary area of disagreement centered around the role she assumed I would play and her total and complete disregard for the possibility that anything different from her perspective could be acceptable. Maybe you can answer this for me better than she did. What does her dream schedule say about her thoughts towards my ministry and the role I was to play in the relationship if it were to advance?

The Weekly Itinerary For The Girl Mark *Almost* Dated

1. Preach Across The Country
2. Sing Around The World
3. Do Book Tours Around The Galaxy
4. Spend Time In Studio Recording Something For #2.
5. Write Books To Sell For #3
6. Pursue Advanced Degree
7. Run A Counseling Center
8. Check In On The Children
9. Be A Wife...If Time Permits

   What's most insightful and troubling is that she never even noticed the intent behind my line of questioning that produced these answers which reveals just how disconnected we can be when we are only focused on ourselves and the furtherance of our agenda. What would've happened if I hadn't said anything? What if I'd ignored the glaring, bright red, effervescent, blinking warning signs and just focused on how attractive she was hoping that the rest would "just work out"? I can tell you exactly what would have happened: we would have ended up in a situation where we were in constant competition as a result of unrealistic expectations concerning roles. The underlying assumption that her ideal schedule revealed is that my purpose and assignments would be insignificant enough that they would naturally take a back seat to hers. For example, her dream of being gone every week would require me to be home every week. Ultimately, that part of my mandate would be unfulfilled.

Keep in mind, this is not to tell you what role you are supposed to play, but this is designed to make sure you realize that tension is bound to ensue if there is not clarity going in about each person's role. In short, expecting someone to fill a role they're not equipped or willing to fill is not unrealistic, but it is downright unfair.

Chapter Four
Live, Learn & Let Go

"Therefore if any person be in a new relationship, let them be a new creature: they didn't do the old things that are passed away; behold, let them start new."

II Mark 4:33

Aren't you glad that's over? I mean, really really glad that it's over? Of course, I know you didn't feel that way immediately after it happened, but looking back on the situation you have to be glad that it's over with now.

None of us relish the feelings of hurt, embarrassment, frustration, or (arguably worst of all) disappointment of knowing you've wasted your time that often accompanies the end of a relationship. Yet, in many situations, when we look back and evaluate the experience, we are glad that it is behind us. We can usually point to several lessons we learned through the experience. Even if the relationship did not end on our terms or at our urging, the hurt tends to subside after a while. What we must avoid, however, is the tendency that many people have of allowing hurt from past relationships to linger longer than it should.

Of course, the initial reaction to that statement would typically be to express how ludicrous it is to think that anyone would knowingly prolong pain. I would have to agree. I am convinced, however, that there are many who unintentionally allow hurt to last longer than it has to as a result of allowing the person who caused the hurt to retain a presence in their life or continue to manifest in new relationships. Regardless of the circumstances surrounding their exit, if someone has left your life and either vowed to never return or caused you to vow that they'll never return, you must allow them to stay gone.

One of the many reasons this is so important is because whenever we allow an old relationship or the negative effects of it to dominate our thinking, we run the risk of punishing the new person God sends for the mistakes of the old person God of which helped us get free.

Contrary to popular belief, a successful relationship is not the result of two people searching all over for the one person who can "complete" them. This line of thinking implies that for whatever reason, both parties are somehow incomplete when they meet. This line of thinking is extremely problematic. The reason for that is because it sanctions the idea that it is someone else's job to complete you, when in reality, you owe it to yourself and your potential partner to come to the table complete.

My father communicated this idea to me better than anyone else I've ever heard. He told me that, "half of a man + half of a women = a whole mess." Why is this crucial to the development of this chapter? Simple. Too many of us do not understand that one of the main reasons we aren't whole and are seeking someone to complete us is because we enter into new relationships while pieces of us are still sitting on the proverbial mantelpieces of old partners.

It is equally detrimental to allow too many pieces of previous relationships to stay in our heart because this can prevent us from giving the new person the chance that they deserve. There are several reasons why we allow this to happen. The first one is the fact that many times, we can't let old relationships go because there is a "soul tie" anchoring us there. There are some cases when we don't even know we're anchored. Understanding the impact that soul ties can have on us is the first step in making sure we don't abort potential relationships because of an unhealthy connection to old relationships.

Contrary to the idea of being equally yoked that we dealt with earlier, soul ties have a very different connotation. Both of these ideas speak to and imply a certain connection, but the purpose and origin of those connections are polar opposites. Those who are equally yoked are bound together for the cause of pursuing a common purpose, while those who are in soul ties are often in bondage as a result of pursuing common pleasure. Soul ties factor so heavily into this discussion because what we often don't even realize is that they prevent us from engaging in new healthy relationships by keeping us stuck in the unhealthy ones of the past. While we could spend an entire book expounding on the perils of soul ties alone, suffice it to say that if someone else is influencing your soul, emotions, thoughts, or will you may be tangled up in a soul tie. I wish I could tell you that breaking free from them was a simple task, but that's simply not the case. They often evolve and strengthen over the course of time with the help of unwise decisions coupled with mutual pursuit.

What I can tell you, however, is that while breaking free from them may be difficult, it is absolutely doable. If you want to be free to engage in new positive relationships, you must sometimes weaken the existing soul tie by not simply parting ways with the individual, but also by parting ways with their articles of affection. One of the greatest dangers posed by soul ties is that they don't even require contact with the person on the other end to exist. They can feed off of memories.

Can we go there for a moment? Good. I'm so glad that you've stopped sleeping with them. That is absolutely crucial to being free from that soul tie and becoming the person God wants you to be as well as positioning yourself to attract the person He wants you to be with. As necessary and productive as that step is, don't tell me you really want to be free from that soul tie if you refuse to stop sleeping with their teddy bear or in their t- shirt. It's great that you no longer take their calls because you know they aren't good for you, but you aren't really serious about breaking that soul tie if you still have the picture from the last vacation you two took together as your screensaver, or if your ringtone is the melody of the song that you both identified as "yours".

Remember, soul ties feed off of a steady diet of memories that reinforce the knot, so if you want freedom, you must not simply stop creating new memories, but you must also begin to distance yourself from the existing memories already created. Let me reiterate this one more time, it is absolutely impossible to be fully available for the one God is sending if their spot is still occupied by someone God ran away. If you're closing the door to that detrimental relationship, shut it completely, lock it, push a dresser in front of it, douse the door with an accelerant, crawl out the back window, set the whole thing on fire, run away from the scene, and never look back.

While a willingness to be free from soul ties is an essential step towards being open to a new relationship that will be free from the negative influences of past relationships, it is certainly not the only step. In fact, if you are truly serious about not making someone new suffer for the mistakes of someone old, you must make sure the new person isn't the old person in disguise. One of the things that always baffles me is the ability of some people to bounce from relationship to relationship and ultimately choosing a person who is just like the ones before. Sure, their name, appearance, background, education, and a host of other factors may be different from that of the previous person, but at the end of the day, the core of who they are ends up proving to be the same.

Have you ever encountered someone like that? Regardless of how much disdain they express for the person who hurt them or how adamantly they vow to never be with someone like that again, they almost always end up with a different manifestation of the same person. What does that really suggest about those who end up in the same situation over and over again? One cannot ignore the commitment that some people have made to ignoring danger signals or red flags at all cost. Sometimes, we are guilty of asking Jesus to be a fence, but then insist jumping over it. Of course, there are those who find themselves in similar predicaments because of their unwillingness to wait and the subsequent rushing that comes as a result of being too eager. In fact, there are several things that play a part in this, but in my opinion, they all seem to center around or at least stem from the issue of self-esteem. Self-esteem, much like experience or culture, is something everyone has to varying degrees. It's not an issue of whether or not someone has self-esteem, but it's an issue of what the self-esteem they have looks like. This is crucial to our subject because the fact of the matter is that many singles fail to realize that we date, mate, and relate on the level of our self- esteem.

Spend some time with that thought while looking back over your own life experiences and observations. Let me talk to the guys for a moment, have you ever seen an absolutely gorgeous lady with a gentleman who left a lot to be desired in your opinion and thought to yourself "How in the world did HE end up with HER?!" What about you ladies? Have you ever seen a man that you considered to be absolutely perfect walking hand-in-hand with a lady you didn't think would have even stood a chance with him? Well, now you know how that happened. They selected someone on the level of their self- esteem. While you may not think they're qualified to be with the person they're with for whatever reason, it really doesn't matter...because they think they're qualified. Now that you've considered outside examples, turn the mirror on your own relationship history for a moment. Does it make sense to you now? I thought it would.

Break The Cycle

Using this information, it becomes easier to see how some people can fall into the same relationship cycles over and over again in spite of a desire not to do so. Sometimes, low self- esteem can cause us to make decisions that are detrimental to our destiny because on some level, we don't really believe we can do better than what we're doing or even deserve better than what (or who) we currently have. Part of the problem with making decisions that are rooted in low self-esteem is that they often prove to be repetitive. It is difficult for someone to see themselves in a better position than the one they're in right now. Some of you are reading this and trying to figure out why you've dated the same person in different forms and the answer is simple. Your choices in people won't change until the way you choose to view yourself changes.

While we have laughed at various points in the book so far and will surely laugh some more before the book is finished, the issue of domestic violence is no laughing matter. It is a problem that affects individuals of all races, backgrounds and socioeconomic statuses. While I dare not attempt to oversimplify an issue as complex and multifaceted as this, there is an observation I must mention. I have personally known several people who were unfortunately trapped in a cycle of selecting abusive partners, and I could not understand for the life of me how it was possible for them to choose people who had the same issue over and over again. From the outside looking in, some of the ill-informed questions I so desperately wanted to ask were, "Didn't you see the warning signs?! Why didn't you ask better questions up front? You didn't look at their previous relationships?" As much sense as these questions made to me, however, it was not until I factored in the role that self-esteem plays in our decisions that I better understood how repeatedly choosing a person with the same issue was even possible. Sometimes not paying attention to warning signs or rushing into things can certainly play a part in a pattern of poor decisions, but the impact of self-esteem cannot be ignored. Let me reiterate, it is never the fault of the victim, but the abuser who preys on low self-esteem.

How we view ourselves is directly connected to how we view what we deserve. Sometimes we pick people who have the same issues because we haven't stopped seeing ourselves in the same negative light. To avoid making the new person suffer for the mistakes of the old person, you must first ensure that you aren't picking the same person again. The first step towards doing this is changing how you see yourself which could result in you either realizing that you deserve better or realizing that you need to be better. After evaluating your self-esteem and elevating your expectations for both yourself and your partner, you then must examine other factors that could prevent you from punishing the new person for the mistakes of the old person.

Now that you've made sure the soul ties are gone and your self-esteem is not holding you back, you have to commit to allowing the new person to be free from the negative consequences that the last person's actions merited. As bad as I want to tell you that this is easy to do, that is simply not the case. There's a popular adage that states "a burnt child dreads the fire" and the sentiment of that statement perfectly conveys my point. It would be beyond insensitive to suggest that you aren't supposed to use the past as a learning experience, but I am suggesting that you do not want to allow it to evolve from a learning experience to an expected experience. As difficult as it may be, however, it is imperative that you allow each person you encounter to prove themselves without the constant and unfair comparisons to a person they most likely have nothing to do with.

Part of what makes adopting this mindset so difficult is that it flies in the face of our natural human penchant for self-preservation. God has placed within each of us what can most simply be described as a desire to stay alive and free from pain at any cost. It is this commitment to self-preservation that makes the earlier statement that "a burnt child dreads the fire" resonate so much within us. Nobody wants to experience pain, but even those of us who have matured to the point of knowing that pain is a necessary part of life don't desire to continually experience it and especially not the same pain. When we fail to make the decision not to see the person who hurt us previously in every new relationship, however, we run the risk of beginning to see things that may not be there. To put this in perspective, let's consider a woman who has the experience of being in a relationship with someone who we would all consider a "mama's boy." It is perfectly reasonable for her to note certain similarities and recognize them when she sees them in new people. At the same time, however, it is absolutely unreasonable to accuse him of being "just like so and so" and vowing to "never be hurt again" just because he called his mother...on Mother's day.

Again, I am not at all advocating for you to completely forget the past and the invaluable lessons it taught you because that would be foolish and irresponsible on your part. You went through what you went through as a part of your development, and you certainly do not want to dismiss that. At the same time, you do not want your fear of being hurt again to smother any possibility of you finding and contributing to a positive, healthy relationship.

Some of you reading this right now are genuinely trying to agree with what I'm saying, you really, really are. However, you can't get around your history of experiences. Some of you are at a point where you don't really believe it's possible to give anyone a fair shot because you aren't fully convinced that what you've seen isn't all there is to see. In other words, some of you have been through so much unhappiness that it's becoming easier and easier to generalize all men as dogs, cheaters, lazy, afraid of commitment, etc., or all women as gold diggers, manipulative, insecure, etc. To reiterate my position once again, I am not at all suggesting that you dismiss these feelings entirely because they play a part in helping you identify danger signs moving forward. In that regard, they are useful. The usefulness of those feelings end when we allow them to completely take over.

Consider this with me for a moment. It is safe to assume that all of us who are reading this have had the unfortunate experience of seeing a motor vehicle accident on the highway at some point in our lives. As disturbing as the sight of a wreck is, I would suggest that none of you made a vow to never ride in a car again after seeing that accident. The reason for this is because even though you considered it unfortunate, you realized that it was, in fact, an accident and you kept on driving. Furthermore, because you're smart, you most likely viewed the accident you saw as a reminder that you should be careful, and pay attention to the signs on the road. This is the same approach we need to take in managing our relationships and balancing the hurt we've experienced with the potential happiness that we could experience. In the same way, we don't allow every car accident we see to keep us off the road, we cannot allow relationships that turned out to be "wrecks" to cause us to vow to never enter another one. We must view them as independent instances that we grow from and reminders to make sure we are not only on the right road but also paying attention to the signs that are all around us. It is crucial that you do not allow the events of the past, no matter how painful or disappointing they may be, to control your future. When you punish new people for the mistakes of others, you allow the person who hurt you to control you.

Chapter Five
The Thirst is Real

*"Jesus wept...because there were so many thirsty
people throughout the land."*

In Matthew 5:6, Jesus informs us, *"Blessed are they
which do hunger and thirst after righteousness: for
they shall be filled"*...but let me help you, He didn't
mean THAT kind of thirst.

I can guarantee you that He was not sanctioning the
type of "thirst" we often reference today to denote
someone who, according to the urban dictionary, is
"too eager to get something" or "desperate." Yeah,
that's not what He meant at all. While Jesus informs us
those who thirst for righteousness are guaranteed to
be filled or satisfied, if you will, He does not offer the
same advice for singles who thirst after other people.
In fact, not only does Jesus not guarantee anything for
thirsty singles, neither does Abraham, Isaac, Jacob,
Rahab, Moses, David, Bathsheba, any of the Major
Prophets, any of the Minor Prophets, Malachi, the
woman at the well, the woman with the issue of blood,
blind Bartimaeus, Paul, Silas, the Philippian Jailer,
John the Baptist, John the Methodist, John the

Pentecostal, John the Revelator or anyone else in the Bible.

The fact of the matter is that the very nature of the term "thirsty" goes hand in hand with the concept of desperation and the only person that desperation appeals to is The Lord. When we consider the nuances associated with being desperate, it often invokes the feelings that accompany being annoyed, nagged, or uncomfortable. Quite frankly, these are feelings no one wants to experience. What makes the issue of being designated as "thirsty" so troubling is that there is no set criterion to actually describe what it looks like. The definition of what kind of behavior is considered thirsty or not is extremely relative and changes based on whom you ask. We can all agree that desperation is like the stench of a cheap cologne that hits you before the person wearing it enters the room and lingers long after they've left. While you may be unable to fully define what being thirsty actually looks like, you regard it almost the same way Supreme Court Justice Potter Stewart regarded pornography. In the 1964 case of Jacob Ellis V. Ohio he stated while he couldn't define what pornography was, he said, "I know it when I see it." With this in mind, let's consider two areas of focus that can help us either properly identify thirstiness in others...or possibly in ourselves.

BOUNDARIES ARE OUR FRIENDS

The first warning sign we should look for while trying to identify desperation or thirstiness is a disregard for healthy boundaries. If there is only one fact that you learn from this chapter, I pray that it's the idea that boundaries are our friends. In fact, say it with me this time, "Boundaries are my friend." Got it? Good. Adopting the proper perspective of boundaries can prevent you from a great deal of heartache and danger in both the short term and long run. The reason for this lies in understanding while boundaries may initially seem like barriers between you and what you desire, they are actually in place for your protection and being able to recognize that difference is a matter of maturity. To illustrate this point, consider the speed limits on our roads and major highways and the way you viewed them as a teenager compared to how you view them now.

If you are anything like me, at one point and time you viewed them as hindrances in place to keep you from enjoying your newfound freedom. If the speedometer goes to 160 MPH, why should we be relegated to only going 45 or 60 MPH? To an immature person, it would seem that the limits are there for no other reason than to unnecessarily hold you back, but a mature person has a different perspective. Maturity helps you understand the limits or boundaries are in place for your protection more than your punishment.

This is the same light in which we have to view the boundaries in our own relationships. They are not there to hinder us but rather to protect us from danger and prevent unwanted heartache, attention, or discomfort. They serve as barriers between our heart or our personal space and those who desire to have access to them. Part of what makes those we consider thirsty so undesirable is their inability to understand this truth. One of the easiest ways to determine if someone is being thirsty or even evaluate whether or not you are on the brink of crossing over into that territory yourself is by examining the way boundaries are respected. If you have not granted someone permission to enter certain areas of your life, their repeated attempts to "break in" are violations of the boundaries you have set in place.

Some of you are undoubtedly raising the question of how exactly does one express interest without crossing boundaries? How can you be granted access into someone's world if you don't take an initial step in that direction? To be fair, that is an extremely valid question, but the answer is found in this truth; interest is only viewed as desperation when it is not mutual. In other words, a man who sends flowers to a woman's place of employment is almost guaranteed to make that woman smile and view him fondly...IF she has a certain level of interest in him or at least an openness to developing one. If the woman has absolutely zero interest in that man, however, that same action with those same flowers is almost guaranteed to cause him to be viewed as "thirsty"...and borderline "stalkerish" for knowing where she works. Mutual interest is the determining factor on whether or not someone's attempts are welcomed or rejected. How do you know if the interest is mutual? I'm so glad you asked. Here are just a few questions you can ask yourself to help make that determination.

1. Who reaches out more?

One of the easiest and most obvious ways to determine if interest is mutual or not is to take the time to examine who initiates contact first on a regular basis. This is such an effective tool in identifying interest because it helps reveal how often you're on the other person's mind. Now there is a caveat that must be mentioned, and that is this tool becomes most effective after a certain level of comfort has been reached between both parties. In other words, I am a firm believer that while the man should initiate the contact, (let me say that again, the man should initiate the contact) once communication has begun, you can gauge the other parties interest by how often they contact you without prompting.

There is a major difference in a call...and a call back, an inbox message...and a reply to an inbox message, a text...and a text back. One of them says "I want you to know I'm thinking about you" while the other says "I want you to know that I'm at least courteous enough to respond back after you've let me know you're thinking of me."

Understanding that difference can mean everything. In short, if you find yourself in a situation where you are always reaching out first, there's a very strong possibility that the other party may not be as interested as you are.

2. Who drives the conversation?

Have you ever had that uncomfortable feeling of running into someone in public who knows you from years ago...but you can't really remember who they are? Have you experienced that weird half conversation where you're really just attempting to be courteous while trying to figure out exactly who this person is? Or, how about when it's someone you recognize but weren't exactly thrilled about running into? Can you take your mind back to that choppy, half-hearted effort you gave at holding a conversation while secretly thinking of ways to make the awkwardness stop? If so, then you know exactly how it feels when attempting to hold a conversation with someone who isn't as interested in you as you are in them. While they may be polite, you will find yourself raising all of the questions, making all of the subject changes, and trying to perform social CPR on a conversation that is quickly approaching code blue status.

3. How deep do their questions go?

I don't think we place enough importance on the types of questions that are asked by a person we are considering as a potential partner. We will go into greater detail about questions in a little bit, but generally speaking, dissecting the questions that are being asked is a phenomenal way of determining if mutual interest is there. Think about it this way, the questions that come out of someone's mouth when talking to you is indicative of the thoughts that are in their mind when thinking of you. Do you see how this can be an invaluable tool in gaining insight into someone's thought processes? Do they ever ask you about your family background or what life looked like for you when you were growing up? Do they ever inquire about your vision and life goals? Are they interested in knowing your opinions on social issues or causes? Or, are they too busy telling you about themselves and asking you elementary "favorite" questions like what's your favorite color, movie, holiday, etc. You must keep in mind that surface level questions reveal surface level thoughts and intentions. I cannot exaggerate the importance of paying attention to what you're being asked because the questions they ask you also reveal what they admit they don't know about you already.

One of the most frustrating things that a person who knows they aren't shallow can experience is the feeling of meeting someone who acts like they already have them all figured out. This approach is actually insulting because it completely dismisses the uniqueness and intricacies of who you are. If they feel they don't have to ask any insightful questions because they have you already figured out based on what they see on social media or from a distance, let them stay at a distance. Interest always leads to investigation.

4. Do they make time for you?

One of the common mistakes that singles who are in a one-sided relationship make is assuming the reason they haven't heard from the other party is simply because "they're busy." Not so. First of all, understand that "busy" is a relative term and when someone tells you that they aren't available to do something or be somewhere because they're busy, what they're really saying in many situations is that they're too busy for that or you. They've performed a social cost analysis and determined that the value of what you're offering doesn't outweigh the value of their other options for that same timeslot. To demonstrate this, think about a good parent for a moment. For the sake of illustration, let's pretend that the two of you are long-time friends, they are at work and you call them to ask if they want to meet you at their favorite restaurant for a late lunch. It would be perfectly understandable for them to express they can't leave right now because of their obligations at work. To advance my point, pretend that as soon as the two of you hang up the phone after agreeing to meet up later and catch up, they receive another phone call from their child's elementary school. Unfortunately, this call informs them there has been a terrible accident at the school, and their child is currently being rushed to the trauma center at a nearby hospital. I can almost guarantee that regardless of the work obligations or deadlines that are looming over their head, at the conclusion of that phone call they will leave their desk, grab their keys, and head out to see about the child they love. While this example is extreme and unfortunate, it perfectly expresses the idea that "too busy" is a relative term that depends on who is making the request and the light that you view them in.

How does this play into identifying mutual interest? In the same way that the nature of the call determines one's availability or willingness to literally make oneself available, the level of interest in a relationship determines one's availability, as well. While the two situations are very different, the principle is the same. When someone is legitimately interested in a person, it doesn't matter what time they call, who they're around, what they're doing, how tired they are, or what they may already have planned on that date, a way will be made. In short, when someone is never available to talk to or spend time with you...they're simply not that into you.

It is impossible to know whether or not you are violating boundaries without first identifying whether or not mutual interest exists. If careful consideration of the above questions has led you to believe that the person who has captured your attention may be interested in you, then you have reason to believe the appropriate breach of boundaries (i.e. continued phone calls, requests for dates, etc.) would be welcomed. If the above questions have caused you to realize that you may be alone in wanting to pursue a relationship, then you should decide to respect the boundaries that are in place and continue developing a friendship.

The reason interest plays such a vital role in the discussion of "thirst" is because it has significance at every level of a budding relationship. What you must understand is being "thirsty" can prevent interest from developing but it can also prevent it from being sustained once it has been developed. Evaluating how you respect boundaries is the first step in determining whether or not you may be perceived as desperate but the second step is all about patience. One of the surest ways to cause someone to lose interest in you and

Mark Moore, Jr.

simultaneously label you as "thirsty" is to be too impatient with the process. Maybe you're not sure whether or not you're thirsty or maybe you have someone who's pursuing you, and you can't quite identify why you're hesitant to move forward, but you don't want to accuse them of acting desperate without good reason. Whatever the case may be, you must remember that patience is more than a virtue, but it's also an excellent indicator of "thirst."

The reason I highlight this is because many people unknowingly ruin friendships that could potentially evolve into more by rushing and pushing for commitments too soon as a result of impatience. To illustrate this, let me revisit the importance of questions which we began to address earlier. While the right questions can play a great role in both determining someone else's level of interest as well as conveying your own, they must be used in the right way and at the right time. Asking the right questions at the wrong time or asking the wrong questions at any time can cause you to lose the interest of the person from whom you've tried so hard to gain it. While you want them to convey your level of interest, you do not want the questions you ask to unintentionally convey a sense of impatience or an uncomfortable urgency. You've finally convinced her to go on a date with you? That's phenomenal, and we are all very proud of you. You asked her what the two of you should name your firstborn child while on that first date? Well, I certainly hope you enjoyed yourself that time because I'm pretty sure it's the last time. After finally asking you for your number yesterday, he texted you to inform you that he was "Just thinking about u"? You go girl. You responded by saying "Awwwww! And I JUST asked God 2 give me a sign concerning who my husband is!"? You go girl...right to that corner over there and have a seat because you're doing too much.

These examples, while extreme, capture the essence of impatience. No one wants to be forced to handle the pressure that is often associated with dealing with someone who seems to be in too much of a hurry. Whenever impatience is introduced into the equation, it tends to raise several red flags and primarily the question of why are they in such a hurry anyway?! Before you get busy crossing certain questions off of your "First Date Agenda," keep in mind impatience manifests not only in the form of questions that are ill-timed but also in the form of commitments that are pursued too soon. Whether we want to admit it or not, one of the quickest ways to scare someone off is by attempting to establish titles or garner a commitment from them before they're ready. It shows an unwillingness to invest time in actually learning who the person is as well as a total disregard for their comfort level. In addition to this, people who are impatient at the beginning of a relationship often tend to be people who don't truly value commitment. This is easy to understand if you consider the fact that those who really value and understand the significance of commitments do not rush into them.

As a leader in my church, for example, I always get excited when new people walk down the aisle and decide they want to join our church family. Without fail you can see people standing and clapping all around the sanctuary with wide smiles on their faces because joining the church is always a cause for celebration. As happy as I am when families or individuals decide to make that commitment, there are two groups of people who join which solicits two types of reactions from me. The first group consists of those who join while visiting for the first time on that particular day. They have never been to one of our worship services before, nobody knows their name just yet, and they don't know anything about the ministry aside from what they've experienced in that particular service and what they may have seen on the website or through social media.

The other group that joins is made up of those who have been visiting the church for a while. These are the ones who have attended multiple services over a span of time and have taken the time to inquire about the ministry. Those who join from this group are typically familiar with other members by name because they've stayed after the end of service long enough to socialize with people and develop relationships. Again to be perfectly clear, I celebrate everyone who steps forward regardless of which group I consider them to be in...but I only get excited about those from the second group. The reason for this is history has shown me that those who make an emotional and impulsive decision to join something as significant as a church without taking the time to actually learn what the church is all about, where it's going, or what it even believes in is someone who will leave just as quickly and unexpectedly as they came. This is the same emotion we can potentially convey if we push for "relationship membership" too soon. It can cause them to feel we aren't really taking the time to get to know them which can also cause them to feel that you don't really value commitment and could be prone to rush out just as easily as you rushed in.

If you have determined after reading the above information and answering the questions that were posed that you might have unintentionally come across as thirsty in the past or you may be doing it even now, fret not. It doesn't make you a bad person, it doesn't mean you will never be fulfilled, and it really doesn't even mean that your current situation has to be permanent. It simply means that you may be eligible to run for president of the "Bro/Sis" Zone and before you even ask, yes, it is exactly what it sounds like...the spiritual equivalent of the Friend Zone. It is the place where the one you want to call "Bae" calls you "Bro." It's the place where church hugs are always accompanied by two quick pats on the back (upper/shoulder area, never lower back). While conveying a sense of desperation is a great way to be placed here, keep the following information in mind.

The way that desperation or "thirst" is defined is a matter of opinion, and there are no absolutes when it comes to how the person you're interested in may perceive anything. Never lose sight of the fact that one relationship does not make or break you. If you feel that being with a particular "them" will, it is important that you step back and evaluate the way you see yourself. It is important you understand your value and worth before you pursue anyone, even if you're going to pursue them the right way. There is absolutely nothing wrong with you for desiring to be a part of a healthy, Godly relationship. In fact, we were designed by God to be relational creatures that draw necessary elements for our social survival through our connections with other people. Don't miss out on those connections by appearing too eager for them. Respect boundaries, allow mutual interest to develop, don't rush the process, ask the right questions at the right time, and most of all...remain prayerful. If you do, I can't guarantee that you will land the person of your dreams, but I can guarantee that you will be a lot less likely to make them file a restraining order against you.

Chapter Six
The Internet is of the Devil

"No relationship formed exclusively online shall prosper."

II Mark 8:32

I f the Bible is right when it says the enemy comes to steal, kill and destroy, like we know that it is, then I am pretty sure the Internet is one of his primary instruments of choice. I mean, if you really take the time to think about it, what other avenue allows as much debauchery to be distributed on such a wide scale with little effort? Of course, someone could make the argument that television is a contender for that spot, but unlike television, the Internet is not bound by scheduling choices or cable provider options. In all fairness, we cannot ignore that there is a great deal of positive that has been made possible as a result of the Internet.

It has aided us in the dispersion of information which has led to advances in technology, medicine, education, public health, entertainment, politics, and essentially every other industry you can think of. Not to minimize the positive effects that it has had on countless secular industries, I don't think the role it has played in advancing the gospel can be exaggerated.

The Internet has allowed the good news of Jesus Christ to reach the four corners of the world at a rate and ease that not long ago would have been considered impossible.

The paradox created by the Internet lies in the fact that the very things that make it such a positive thing are the same things that make it dangerous. The relative ease of access to it, its limited restrictions and corresponding workarounds, and its never-ending supply of information make it both a potential blessing and curse. What stands out most in my mind is the fact that the Internet only requires you to make a connection and once that connection has been made, you can go anywhere you want to go, see anything you want to see, and learn anything you want to learn. What's most dangerous for those who are in the process of pursuing a relationship, however, is the fact that the Internet also allows people to be who or whatever they want to be.

This is part of the reason the Internet plays such a unique role in our modern-day relationships. It would be beyond impossible to write a book for singles in this generation without acknowledging the various ways the Internet impacts them. From the myriad of dating sites there are to the tendency that some people have to convert every social media platform into a dating site, the Internet is a key player in the relationship game. For the purpose of understanding my premise and the thought process behind this particular chapter, I would ask you to consider the Internet as "digital currency" for a moment. If you are like me, you have heard many people make the argument that money changes people. It is often used to suggest that sweet, selfless, considerate people are somehow transformed by the newfound acquisition of resources or wealth. I am of the opinion that while this theory is widely circulated, it is not entirely true. My belief is money doesn't change anyone at all, but rather it simply allows them an opportunity to afford to be who they've been all along.

In the same way that money or tangible currency takes on the personality of its owner, our digital currency operates in the same exact manner. The Internet simply gives you the chance to finally afford to be who you really are by providing you with a platform to show your true self to the world. In other words, the Internet, and more specifically social media, have never made anyone messy, deceptive, manipulative, or any of the other negative traits that we, unfortunately, see so frequently online through social media. It has allowed messy people to show the messiness that has been there all along.......All of these things factor into why I am completely convinced, beyond a shadow of a doubt, that when it comes down to the development of our relationships, the Internet is of the devil.

I want to provide you with several supporting facts to further explain my position, but we must begin with the understanding that any relationship that exists in this day and age will, in fact, be touched by the long arm of the Internet. It plays far too great of a role in our modern lives, in general, to not influence our relationships. That is something we cannot control. What we can control, is the degree to which we allow it to influence us, as well as the impact it has on our actions, interactions, and reactions. If you are not aware of the fact that the Internet will play a role in any relationship you develop, whether it is platonic or potentially romantic, then you will be caught off guard when the time comes for you to manage it. The way you decide to manage how the Internet factors into your relationships is extremely important because the ramifications of mismanaging it could be so severe.

There was once a time when ruining a relationship or reputation for that matter actually required a little bit of effort. You had to physically be in the wrong place at the wrong time, or you had to actually get in your car, drive somewhere you shouldn't be, and do something that you shouldn't have. Now, unlike then, all it takes to ruin a relationship is a lapse in judgment and the click of a button or two. The internet has the potential to make poor decision-making so much easier. Because of this, I must share two things that must be kept in mind after first acknowledging the role our online decision making makes in our relationships.

STOP TELLING THE WORLD YOUR BUSINESS

One of the greatest threats that our online presence poses to our real-life relationships is the wide range of opportunities it provides for us to overshare. From Facebook posts to Instagram photos, our social media platforms give us endless opportunities to express our full spectrum of emotions and offers very little guidance as to what *too much* actually is. Not only can social media offer us space to share absolutely whatever is on our mind, but I would suggest that social media culture encourages us to make constant attempts at achieving shock value. You can see the results of this by simply considering that everything on social media is fueled by the affirmation and attention of others. We can try to provide a well-worded explanation for our posting and attempt to attribute it to some intrinsic need to encourage others through our words (or something along those lines), but at the end of the day, one of the main reasons we post is to receive likes, shares, retweets, and views.

Chances are you can think of a few "like junkies" in your office, classroom, or family who are constantly checking their phones to see how many likes or comments their most recent selfie (never mind the fact that it's the same pose and outfit as the one they posted an hour ago) received. Oh, you can't think of anyone like that? Well, there's a strong possibility that somebody is thinking about *you*. Because of this mass addiction to likes, people are constantly striving to provide content that is, for lack of a better term, "likeable." I wish I could tell you that the quickest and easiest way to garner likes online was through posting positive, uplifting content that didn't possess a trace of negativity, but that wouldn't be entirely true. While the occasional video of a cat playing the piano or a toddler doing cartwheels is bound to cross our timelines, far too often they are sandwiched between videos of violent fights, cruel pranks, and the embarrassing moments of others. The unfortunate fact of the matter is the things that tend to capture people's attention are those things that can be considered sexy or sensational; dramatic or debatable; confrontational or critical. It seems that in far too many instances the picture of the low-cut graduation party outfit gets more likes than the picture of the actual degree. Or, the post about the scandal collects more comments than the article about the community give back. The consistent posting of these negative things is an indication of our generation's willingness to show whatever will bring attention, be it positive or negative.

As popular as drama, sex appeal, violence, and ridicule can be, however; very few things tend to be as captivating to an audience as the personal business of others. The evidence of this can be seen all around us if we would only take the time to look. This phenomenon is so common to us now that we may not even really think about it anymore, but one of the things that make the day and age that we live in so strange is that we have made celebrities out of reality television stars. Think about how utterly ridiculous this is for a moment. There are people walking around who have millions of dollars in their various accounts that we put there in exchange for nothing more than an opportunity to watch them live.

Let that sink in for just a moment. What do the various reality television stars we allow to influence our style, lingo, and perspectives offer us in exchange for the millions of dollars that the attention we give them positions them to make? That's absolutely right, nothing more than the privilege of looking at them.

Take the blatant narcissism out of the equation for a moment and consider how this impacts our relationships and the role the Internet and social media play in them. Many of the same people who account for the millions of views that reality shows get are the same people on your timeline, and their appetite doesn't necessarily change with the platform. Their need for drama and voyeurism, which they try to satisfy through their television choices, translates to their social media platforms as well.

It is at this point we begin to see why over sharing through social media is not only *so easy* but also *so dangerous* to do. The attention you are guaranteed to receive as a result of posting your personal business is tempting, but the light that the information you share can cause you to be viewed in should serve as a deterrent.

Whenever we share too much information online about our relationships or our personal life in general, we invite the opinions of strangers who don't even know us well enough to deserve an opinion. As angry as you may be with "Bae" for example, you should be very careful about broadcasting your displeasure with your timeline and the world. The reasons to exercise discretion and discernment in this situation are numerous, but one of them that you should certainly consider is that by exposing a rift between you and your significant other, you are unintentionally inviting other voices into the equation. Meaning, any devious person who has had their eye on "Bae" for a while now has suddenly been made aware that a door may be open for them to make a move. As unfortunate as it may be to consider, you must realize that all of your online "friends" really aren't your friends, some of your followers are only following in hopes that you'll stumble and some of them have an agenda. To make matters worse, you forfeit the right to be angry with people for being in your business if you've told them your business.

I would be doing you a great disservice if I allowed you to think that you should only consider what you post about your relationship if it is about an argument or a rift because the same warning applies to overwhelming expressions of affection and love. Maybe I am the only one, but I have watched with great confusion as individuals have insisted on posting every single detail their "amazing" relationship. The only problem with this is that I've seen them post this same kind of content...about *too many different people*. One of the greatest threats that over sharing on social media can pose to your potential relationship is that it can cause your stability to be called into question.

The fact of the matter is that some relationships simply do not work out. This is not always your fault or anyone's fault for that matter. What you want to avoid, however, is the appearance of being unstable and jumping from relationship to relationship at the drop of a hat. The reason for this is that even though you may not realize it, what you are accidentally telling the world and quite possibly the one you're supposed to be with is, in addition to having no discretion you also have no discernment. If last week's boyfriend or girlfriend was your soul mate, your rib, and your everything, then why do you have a different one this week? Are you that rash in your decision making that you jump into every possible situation headfirst without taking the time to pray for direction regarding the situation or even to vet the individual who's captured your attention? Will this current person that you're swooning over prove to be the flavor of the month, another flavor of the week, or is this one just the daily special? These are the types of questions that this behavior generates from people when they see that you are once again taking another ride on the relationship carousel.

The fear of being perceived as unstable and inviting too many other bias voices into your relationship should certainly be enough reason to take heed to what your post, but there are still other factors that merit our consideration. Not only do you authorize people to make snap decisions about your stability and relationship history by over sharing, but you also give them the freedom to make judgments about you based on who you've decided to link up with. Have you ever had the experience of looking back at some of the relationship choices you made in the past? Have you ever wondered, "What in the world was I thinking? How did I miss so many warning signs?" Here's the thing. It doesn't take everybody as long as it took you to see it. Some people are already aware of all the negative traits about the person you have been championing. In other words, while you may have just learned that he's arrogant, there are others who have known this for years and now feel that *arrogant* must be your type. You just learned she doesn't wash the back of her neck? Well, guess what, there's someone else who's sat behind her in church before and seen her shirt collar. Now, they think you like dirty necks. Since it's just you and I talking right now, I will confess something to you as long as you promise not to judge me. Deal? Okay then. Here it is.

There have been some wonderful ladies that have crossed my path and completely captured my attention that I lost interest in and stopped pursuing the moment I learned who they dated previously. Truth be told, they were perfect for me on paper. They had all of the physical specifications I asked The Lord for, the right educational, family, and of course spiritual background. We even shared some similar interests. What proved to be the deal breaker for me, however, was discovering who else they considered a good match for them at one time. Before you attribute this decision to some false interpretation of some "guy code," allow me to assure you that it had nothing to do with that. In short, my decision was simply the result of stepping back and analyzing the situation which led me to the conclusion that if she was happy with *that*, there was no way she would fit with *this*. Is it entirely fair for people to assess you by your past decisions? I would say not entirely. Is it real? Absolutely.

Make a conscious effort to not scare away your *tomorrow* by being too careless in the selection of your *today*. It is easy to fall victim to our society's tendency to overshare, especially when there is so much pressure not to appear like you've been left behind. What you cannot do, however, is allow the frustration of always being the bridesmaid and never the bride or always the groomsman and never the groom cause you to settle for someone who is less qualified and about as mature as the flower girl or the ring bearer. You should be mindful of what you post concerning your relationships not only for fear of it not working out, but because everybody doesn't have to know everything. Choose wisely, post carefully, and be prayerful about every decision...because you never know who's evaluating your choice.

STOP FALLING IN LOVE WITH AVATARS

By now, I certainly hope that you are beginning to see the various ways that our online decisions can impact and affect our real-life relationships. From the temptation to overshare personal matters on our timelines to the consequences that accompany that, the Internet for all of the positive it offers is a potentially dangerous place for those who are trying to build a relationship. In addition to the importance of not telling the entire world our business, it is equally important that we avoid falling in love with avatars while on online. To avoid confusion with the fictional blue creatures of Hollywood, we will use the following as our working definition of what an avatar is. An avatar is defined as "an icon or figure representing a particular person in Internet forums" or in other words, it is an image that represents you while online. When people look at the profile picture you have selected on your various social media sites, they are actually looking at your avatar or the image you have placed there to represent you.

While this is a technical term in nature, I think that its meaning can be applied on a much larger scale because there are a lot of people today who end up falling in love with nothing more than the online representatives of people they really don't know. It would be easy for us to relegate this to those who have been the victims of what's commonly known as "Catfish" schemes, where people completely fabricate identities and enter relationships under the guise of being someone else entirely. Certainly, that can apply to this as well, but I am more so talking about the tendency that some people have to fall for online representations of people who aren't even necessarily trying to deceive them.

Your first thought when reading that may be to question how it's possible to do this when someone isn't even trying to manipulate you. This is actually easier to do than you may initially believe because of the way online platforms and social media give us a sense of connection with strangers. Anyone who has ever been approached in real life by a social media friend who has introduced themselves by their username understands how this works.

Because social media has introduced us to people's avatars, it is not that difficult to begin to develop a sense of relationship with or even feelings for the representatives of the people we think we actually know. The reason this deserves to be mentioned is because avatars are again, simply representatives of actual people. In other words, what you see of a person online is not actually who they are, it's simply a depiction of who they are. What makes the Internet such a confusing place as it pertains to relationships is that you only see what people show you, and they only show you what they want you to see.

This information helps explain much of the problem associated with falling in love with avatars because it forces you to begin to address the question of whether or not you actually know the person behind the avatar. While our various social media platforms can be extremely helpful in providing us with a snapshot of whom a person is, we must not allow ourselves to develop feelings for the representative. The best possible way that I can explain this is by highlighting the way that Internet connections can foster a false sense of connection when in reality, real, authentic, lasting relationships still require some degree of physical interaction to truly thrive, especially if they are going to be romantic in nature. I am afraid that in the same way text messaging, and our constant quest to shrink complex thoughts into 140 characters or less has butchered the English language, social media has caused us to lose the beauty of human contact.

Basing your level of interest solely on what you know about the representative or avatar without knowing the actual person is a great way to set yourself up to fall in love with the idea of a person and not the actual person.

At this point, I can only hope that my decision to be personal right here won't offend you, but I can't accurately convey this message without giving you unrestricted access into my heart for a moment.

As a young single man, one of my greatest fears is having someone fall in love with the idea of me. If I can be fully transparent, I would like to think that I am a relatively good catch, but what makes me nervous is that by some standards, I am almost an ideal catch and therein lies the problem. For a woman to say that she wants a man who comes from a good family, makes his own money, has traveled the world, has a six-figure education, an entrepreneurial mind, and no children is not the same thing as saying she wants *Mark Moore, Jr.* While I fit those criteria, that list is not all that I am. Therefore, it is entirely possible for someone to want the *idea of me* without actually wanting me at all. Are you with me? Good.

This one question alone should make us use caution when we feel ourselves beginning to develop feelings for people primarily based on what we see online. Be honest with yourself, when it comes to the person whose page you spend all day checking for updates, do you actually know them enough to like them? Or, do you just like the idea of them? In fact, can you really, truly like them without having some idea of how they would interact with you in real life? Whether the answer to that question is yes or no for you, what cannot be debated is the importance of at least being aware that the possibility exists. You owe it to yourself and the person you're considering to make sure that it's them you're interested in and not simply the idea that they represent to you.

In and of itself, the Internet and more specifically social media has absolutely no character. Much like money, it takes on the personality of its owner. It is important that you make sure you're not guilty of jeopardizing your current relationship or preventing your potential one by using it unwisely and sharing too much. You always want to make sure you aren't allowing the false sense of connection it provides to lull you into falling for someone you don't really know. That would be bad for the both of you. If used the right way, social media and other Internet forums can be an absolutely invaluable resource for sharing information and making positive connections, however, if used the wrong way...the Internet is of the devil.

Chapter Seven
You Can't Change Them

"They shall be like a tree planted by the rivers of water...unless of course they decide that they want to move."

II Mark 2:8

I will never forget the words my younger brother, George, uttered one day while we were at our grandparents' home in Belleville, Michigan. At this particular time, George was an energetic three-year-old full of personality, and I was his eight- year-old big brother and boss. Although we are five years apart, our parents (our mother to be more precise) had a habit of dressing us as twins way past the age when it was cute. At any rate, on this particular day, our playtime was interrupted by my grandmother calling George inside because my father was on the phone and wanted to speak with him. I don't know if George thought he was in trouble and that was the reason he didn't want to talk to dad or if he was simply having too much fun to stop playing and go inside. Regardless of the reason, George did not want to talk to dad...at all. This was conveyed in his response to my grandmother when she called him to get the phone. George pondered her statement for a moment, looked at her with the kind of polite defiance that only a three-year-old can get away with, and declared with a calm resolve, *"I can't want to."*

I don't think there's any way he could have realized how profound that statement actually was, nor do I think it could have been any more perfect. Notice, he didn't say, *"I can't"* or, *"I don't want to."* No, those would have been too easy. He said, *"I can't want to."* which was essentially his way of conveying that his commitment to not doing what was being asked of him was so strong, that it wasn't possible for him to even want to do it.

The reason I open with this story is because the sentiment that three-year-old George conveyed in that statement to our grandmother is the exact sentiment that a lot of the people we are attempting to change are conveying to us. It's not that they can't change. It's not that they don't know how to change. They simply *"can't want"* to change and whether you want to hear it or not, *you can't make them.* One of the greatest myths that modern singles have bought into is the myth that suggests that the only reason a particular person hasn't changed yet is because we simply haven't tried hard enough yet. This flawed perspective erroneously places the burden of changing on you, *the one who wants to see the change* instead of *the person who needs to change.* It implies that we somehow have the ability to change people. We sometimes even apply it to people we aren't even in relationship with yet with statements like *"I know that they're _____ now, but they just haven't met me yet."* Or, *"They can't stop _____ yet, but I'll change that when I get ahold of them."* While this sounds admirable, it simply isn't true.

Before you begin to tune me out entirely, let me inform you that I am not at all suggesting that change is impossible in relationships. In fact, there can be no compromise where there is no change. Compromise is a vital ingredient in the recipe for any successful relationship, regardless of its nature. Friends, siblings, and those who date with purpose must compromise. I am also not denouncing the claim that you may be making right now, while reading this, that you know for a fact people can change because you have changed. I dare not argue with the progress you've made, but I would ask you to note the actual claim I make in the title of this chapter. The understanding that I want you to gain through this chapter is not that people can't change, but rather, *you* can't change people. This means we have to identify exactly where this change comes from if we have established that it doesn't come from other people. Essentially, the only people who can change a person are The Lord and that person. And even The Lord is kind enough to allow the person in need of change to make the first move. How does this factor into our relationships? The moment we take the onus for someone else's change off of our shoulders and place it where it belongs is the moment we free ourselves from unnecessary stress and worry. Why is this so important you ask? Great question! Let's examine a few of the reasons.

TIME IS NOT ON YOUR SIDE

One of the greatest hindrances we often run into while attempting to change people is the forgotten factor of time. We seem to think, for whatever reason, because we are as wonderful as we think we are, it's only a matter of time before the issues we don't like in others suddenly change at our urging. We fail to realize that time is not on our side. We must consider the fact that the individual we're expecting to change has spent years becoming what and who they are. So what makes us think they will be able to change what took them 30 years to become in only 30 days? While sobering, this reality has the power to set us free from misguided expectations.

Granted, you may be able to influence or change their preferences, but that's not the same thing as changing the person. To be more specific, you may be able to get someone who is not accustomed to eating healthy to switch to low-sodium seasoning or use an alternative to butter for a while, but until that person decides to change their lifestyle in general, they will continue to have a poor diet and occasionally use, "I Can't Believe It's Not Butter."

IT'S NOT AN INDICTMENT ON YOU

Another problem with thinking that you can change people is the feelings of inadequacy that follow failed attempts. What you must keep in mind, however, is that because it's not your responsibility to make it happen, it's also not your fault when it doesn't happen. Regardless of how bad you may want to see a person change, you don't possess the skills to force it, no matter how great you are. As often as we have laughed together throughout this book, I hope you won't mind if we take a moment here to be serious. I have had conversations with fellow singles that felt, for whatever reason, they possessed the power to somehow love others through some deep internal issues. For example, I've listened to sisters who felt the only reason their boyfriend or potential husband was reputed to be a cheater was simply because she hadn't "put it on him" yet. They were convinced that the remedy for a complex deep-seeded issue like infidelity was found within their loins. My response to that claim has always been to point out that if people cheat on actresses, models, and some of the most beautiful women in the world, what makes you think you are the exception? While I'm on it, no amount or caliber of sex can make them *faithful* if they're not, *straight* if they aren't sure, or *love you* if they don't. This line of thinking further reinforces the flawed idea that the issues other people are facing are somehow your fault and they're not.

Let me reiterate, thinking this way is admirable, but I encourage you to remember that because God promised to never put more on you than you're able to bare, you should make the same commitment. At the end of the day, that person has to want to change, and they, along with the help of God, are the only one that can take their "can't want to" away.

This last truth brings us to a close. We've laughed, been enlightened, and can now walk away with a clearer understanding of dating, its purposes, and effective practices. For many of you, I'm pretty sure that I'm no longer your favorite person, which is absolutely fine, but I guarantee that you'll thank me and remember my warnings before you pursue your next relationship or connection.

My prayer is that you will find the one, or be found by the one God has purposed you to connect with. More than anything, I pray you find overwhelming happiness in being the individual God has created you to be.

About the Author

Mark A. Moore, Jr. is a native of Indianapolis, Indiana, and currently resides in Atlanta, GA. In addition to traveling internationally as a speaker, Mark serves as the Pastoral Assistant of Faith Covenant Church under the leadership of his father, Bishop Mark A. Moore, Sr. He is a graduate of the historical & prestigious Morehouse College, and holds a Bachelor of Arts Degree in Sociology.

Mark is the CEO of Moore Group Enterprises, a company committed to effecting positive change in ministry, media, and the marketplace. He compassionately leverages his influence and knowledge to improve the lives of leaders across the world. He is the founder and host of the Young Leaders Conference, affectionately known as YLC. Since its development, YLC has impacted the lives of leaders from over 36 U.S. states and ten countries.

Among his generation, Mark is quickly emerging as a premier and innovative strategist in the areas of branding, marketing, and leadership development.

STAY CONNECTED

Thank you for purchasing *Boaz is Dead*! Mark would like to connect with you. Below are a few ways you can stay posted on new book releases, speaking engagements, workshops, and more!

INSTAGRAM @mmoorejr
FACEBOOK Mark Moore, Jr.
WEBSITE www.markmoorejr.com
PERISCOPE @mmoorejr
TWITTER @mmoorejr

Made in the USA
Lexington, KY
27 June 2017